BASEBALL

How to Play the All-Star Way

By **Mark Alan Teirstein**

Introduction by **Dave Fleming**

Illustrated by **Art Seiden**

Photographs by **Frank Becerra, Jr.**

★ An **Arvid Knudsen** book ★

RSVP
**RAINTREE
STECK-VAUGHN**
P U B L I S H E R S
The Steck-Vaughn Company

Austin, Texas

Dedication

To my son Jason, who made the greatest catch I ever saw; to my daughter Amanda, a cleanup hitter who comes through in the clutch; to my wife Chatty, who keeps — and knows — the score; to my dad Al, who taught me the game; and to the Blues, who let me play it.

Acknowledgments

Great appreciation for their contributions, inspiration, guidance, and technical support goes to Ron Melancon, Arvid Knudsen, Frank Becerra, Jr., Dave Fleming, Nolan Ryan, Don Mattingly, Tom House, Jeff Idelson, the New York Yankees, John Blake, the Texas Rangers, Dave Aust, the Seattle Mariners, Gerald Blount, Tom Pedulla, Gifford Krivak, Richard Pagliaro, Sheila Margolis, Ellen Lever, Lisa Winston Wilentz, and Mr. Saltzman.

Special thanks to my mother, Alice, for her energy, enthusiasm, and encouragement, and to my grandmother, Anne Sobel, for her inspiration, faith, and devotion.

Photograph on p. 12 and from the collection of the Texas Rangers.
Photograph on p. 38 from the collection of the New York Yankees.
Photographs on pp. 4 and 38 from the collection of Frank Becerra, Jr.
All other photographs from the collection of Arvid Knudsen.

© Copyright 1994, Steck-Vaughn Company

Published by Raintree Steck-Vaughn Publishers, an imprint of Steck-Vaughn Company.

Library of Congress Cataloging-in-Publication Data

Teirstein, Mark Alan
Baseball / written by Mark Alan Teirstein
p. cm. — (How to play the all-star way)
"An Arvid Knudsen book."
ISBN 0-8114-5776-1
1. Baseball—Juvenile literature. [1. Baseball.]
I. Title. II. Series.
GV867.5.T44 1994
796.357—dc20 93-23271 CIP AC

Printed and bound in the United States

1 2 3 4 5 6 7 8 9 0   99 98 97 96 95 94 93

73693

CONTENTS

Dave Fleming was the most successful rookie pitcher in the major leagues in 1992, even though he pitched for a Seattle Mariners team that had the worst record in the American League. Fleming won 17 games and lost only 10. He had an earned run average of just 3.39. He pitched four shutouts. During one stretch, he won nine games in a row.

Fleming's rise to the major leagues was very fast. He reached the Mariners five years after graduating from high school. He signed with Seattle after leading the University of Georgia to the College World Series title. There he had struck out the side in the final inning to clinch the championship.

INTRODUCTION

I was playing for the Mariners' Jacksonville minor league team. I was told to report to the next minor league level, the Triple-A Calgary team. I got on a plane. But I did not make it to Calgary that day. Instead I wound up in the major leagues...

To get to Calgary I had to change planes in Dallas, Texas. But while I was waiting in the Dallas airport, I heard my name over the loudspeaker. There was a phone call for me. When I answered the phone, it was the Mariners. They told me not to get on the plane to Calgary. They told me I was going to the major league team instead. They told me to switch to a plane to California and join the Mariners in time for their game that night against the Oakland Athletics.

I had to wait for two hours in the Dallas airport. No one around me knew I was now a major leaguer. I just sat there with a big smile on my face.

When I got to California, I took a taxi right over to the Oakland stadium. By the time I got there, the game had already started. I could hear the crowd roaring in the stadium while I was in the locker room getting into my uniform. I signed my first major league contract right there while I was getting dressed. I was pulling one leg of my uniform on with one hand while I was signing the contract with the other.

Then I went out to the field, and the manager said to go to the bull pen. To get to the bull pen in Oakland, you have to walk past the stands. I could tell by the way the fans were looking at me that they thought I was like any other major leaguer. They did not know I had just arrived. It gave me a feeling of pride: I had made it quicker than most people thought and quicker than I thought.

Playing in the majors was a dream in the back of my mind when I was growing up. But you never think it is really going to happen. I was just playing with my friends, making new friends, and having a good time.

When I got to high school, I realized that my baseball ability might help give me the chance to get an education in college. Then in college I started to think about playing professionally.

But when you are a kid 10 or 11 years old you shouldn't be planning to play in the major leagues. That is too far off. You should be learning the proper basics of the game — as shown in this book, *Baseball: How to Play the All-Star Way,* by Mark Teirstein. And most of all, you should just have fun, and play every chance you get.

— *Dave Fleming,*
Seattle Mariners

CHAPTER 1

A LITTLE BASEBALL HISTORY

It is a scene that has been repeated for more than 100 years. The batter gets set to face the pitcher. He digs his feet firmly in the dirt. He squeezes the bat handle. He raises the bat above his shoulder. He is like a lumberjack about to swing his ax into a big tree. He is ready to use the bat as his weapon. He must try to hit the ball that the pitcher will soon throw. The pitcher stares at his catcher. The catcher gives him the "sign." The sign is a secret signal. It tells the pitcher what type of pitch to throw. The batter stares back at the pitcher. The batter is looking for any clue that will help him spot the ball. He has to see the ball to hit it. The sooner he sees it the better chance he will have.

For this moment it is just pitcher against batter. Their teammates will spring into action once the pitch is thrown. Major league or Little League, fancy ballpark or in the backyard, one hundred years ago or today, the showdown is the same. The pitcher rocks and fires. The batter strides and swings. Then the game jumps to life with a burst of action and excitement just as it did when the first baseball game was played on the Elysian Fields of Hoboken, New Jersey. It was June 19, 1846, fifteen years before the Civil War.

◀ Nolan Ryan of the Texas Rangers has been named an All-Star eight times.

Alexander Joy Cartwright

Alexander Joy Cartwright gets credit for planning that first game. It was between the Knicker-bockers and the New York Nine. It was played much like a game called "rounders." Rounders was played hundreds of years ago by English soldiers.

The highest level of pro-fessional baseball is called the major leagues. Twenty-eight teams are divided into two groups. Those groups are the American League and the National League. Each team plays 162 games in the regular season. Then there are play-offs. At the end of the season, there is the World Series. The World Series is a showdown between the American League and National League champions. The World Series decides the best team of the year.

The best players of the year play in the All-Star Game. The fans choose the All-Stars. The best players of all time get named to the National Baseball Hall of Fame. Players, managers, and umpires are in the Hall of Fame. Less than 200 players have made it into the Hall of Fame.

The Hall of Fame is located in Cooperstown, New York. It is a fun place to visit for fans of all ages. The Hall of Fame includes Ty Cobb. He holds the record for highest career batting average (.367). Slugger Babe Ruth is in the Hall of Fame. His ability to hit home runs made baseball a popular sport. Hank Aaron is also in the Hall of Fame. Aaron holds the career record for home runs (755). It took him 2,500 more turns at bat than Ruth to break Ruth's long-standing record of 714 homers.

Baseball is a game played mostly by boys and girls. Very few men continue playing the game as professionals. So far no women have made it to the major leagues, although there was a professional women's baseball league, called the All-American Girls Professional Baseball League, between 1942 and 1954.

There are only 700 players in the major leagues. The chances of becoming a major leaguer are very slim. It takes years of practice and hard work. It takes a lot of skill and some luck.

There are numerous youth organizations. The largest is Little League. In 1993 Little League had 180,000 teams in 60 countries. There are 2.6 million Little League players.

Nolan Ryan has been an All-Star eight times. He has pitched a record seven no-hitters. He threw a record 5,668 strikeouts heading into the 1993 season. He is sure to be a Hall of Famer. Ryan offers good advice to young baseball players. "The most important thing," he says, "is to have fun and enjoy it."

Baseball is fun to play.

FINDING A TEAM

Some of the best games are "pickup" games. They are a lot of fun. They are played by friends in a neighborhood field or at a nearby school. There are also many organized leagues. These leagues are grouped by age and skill.

Most town recreation departments have their own leagues and youth programs. If not, the town officials can direct you to the closest youth league. Police departments and schools often sponsor youth leagues. The most well-known and largest youth program is Little League.

There is also a Little League Challenger Division. This is for mentally and/or physically disadvantaged youths ages 6 to 18. In 1993 more than 20,000 youngsters played in the Challenger Division. There were 650 teams in the United States, Canada, and Czechoslovakia. Players with one arm have even reached the major leagues. Pete Gray was an outfielder with one arm. He got 51 hits for the St. Louis Browns in 1945. Pitcher Jim Abbott has been missing his right hand since birth. He won 18 games for the California Angels in 1991 and pitched a no-hitter for the New York Yankees in 1993.

For more information about all Little League programs, contact:

Little League Baseball Headquarters
P.O. Box 3485
Williamsport, Pa., 17701
(717) 326-1921

◄ Jim Abbott, pitcher for the New York Yankees, is one of the most respected players in baseball.

Physical Conditioning

Baseball can be played by anyone of almost any shape, size, strength, or speed. But being in good physical condition will always help you play better. It will also be a safer and healthier experience.

"For every athlete, proper nutrition and proper conditioning play an important role," says future Hall of Fame pitcher Nolan Ryan. Ryan was still pitching in the major leagues at age 46. He pitched his seventh no-hitter at the age of 44.

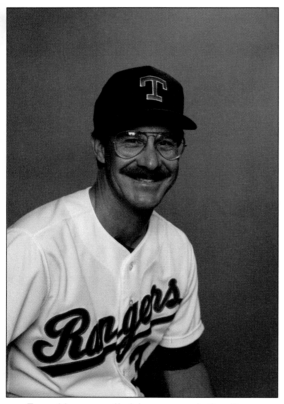

Tom House, pitching coach for the Texas Rangers

Tom House is the pitching coach for the Texas Rangers. He says young players should only do exercises that use their own body weight. "As for training with weights, you should follow the shaving rule," he says. "If you're not shaving yet, you shouldn't be pumping iron." House suggests five exercises for young players: push-ups, pull-ups, chin-ups, sit-ups, and dips.

Equipment

You do not need a lot of equipment to play baseball. But you do need certain items.

The ball: A baseball is the size of an orange. It is covered with horsehide or a similar material. The cover is stitched tightly together. The inside of the ball is made of yarn wrapped around cork or rubber.

Bats: Metal bats are often used in youth leagues, high schools, and colleges. Metal bats do not break easily. They cost more than wooden bats, but they last longer. It is all right to use a wooden bat. In the major leagues only wooden bats are allowed.

Helmet: Every batter must wear an approved helmet. The helmet must be worn when you are batting. It also must be worn once you have reached base. All batters and baserunners must wear a helmet at all times. There are no exceptions. The catcher also wears a helmet.

Protective cup: A protective cup is usually made of hard plastic. It is worn in a form of underwear called an athletic supporter. All male players should wear a protective cup.

Face mask, chest protector, and shin guards: The catcher wears a face mask, chest protector, and shin guards.

Shoes: Players can wear sneakers. Most players wear shoes with hard rubber cleats. These grip the ground just as well as metal spikes. Most youth leagues do not allow metal spikes. Catchers and umpires may also wear special shoes. These shoes have metal toes. They protect against foul tips and pitches in the dirt.

Gloves: All fielders wear a glove on one hand to help catch the ball. The other hand is called the "throwing hand."

There is a different type of glove for each position. The catcher uses a large, almost round glove. It has extra padding. The first baseman uses a long glove. It looks like a lobster claw. The rest of

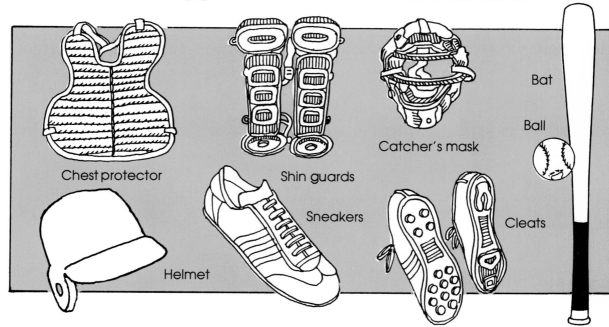

Chest protector

Shin guards

Catcher's mask

Bat

Ball

Sneakers

Cleats

Helmet

the infielders use smaller gloves. These have five fingers and webbing to help catch the ball. Outfielders' gloves look like infielders' gloves, but they are much bigger. Pitchers also use larger gloves.

It is very important to take good care of your glove. When you get a new glove it will be very stiff. It will be hard to close it around a ball. Apply some glove oil. You can get glove oil at any sporting goods store. Work the oil into the leather. Then put a ball in the glove. Wrap the glove tightly with a belt or string. Put it under your mattress for one week. Then use the glove often in practice. It will be "broken in," or ready to use, by the time the season starts.

The care continues after your glove is broken in. Always keep a ball in the glove between games. This will help it keep its molded shape. A good glove becomes a part of you. It is like having a bigger hand at the end of your arm. It should feel like that when you are fielding.

If you take good care of your glove, it will take good care of you. A glove in good condition is definitely an advantage.

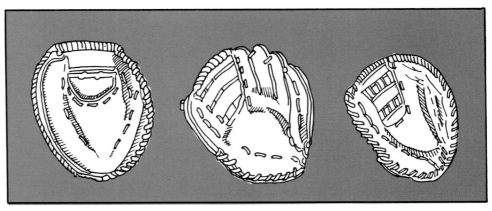

Catcher's mitt   Fielder's glove   First baseman's glove

HOW BASEBALL IS PLAYED

There are many different baseball fields. There are many different players of all ages. But the rules remain the same. The game played by children is almost exactly the same as the game played by adults.

The Field

The size of a baseball field is different for each field. Major league fields are more than 300 feet from home plate to the outfield fence. Some are more than 400 feet to the center field fence. Little League fields are 200 feet from home plate to the outfield fence.

All baseball fields have a general shape in common. They are shaped like a wide slice of pizza. There is a diamond-shaped portion that is called the base path. The base path fits into the small tip of the pizza slice. The area inside the base path is the infield. Outside the base path is the outfield.

There are lines along both sides of the pizza slice. These lines go all the way from the small tip to the fence. They are called foul lines. The field between the foul lines is called fair territory. The area outside the foul lines is called foul territory.

The diamond-shaped base path has a station at each of the four points of the diamond. These are called bases. The base at the tip of the pizza slice is called home plate. It has a different shape from the other bases. The other bases are like square pillows. Home plate is flat and hard.

BASEBALL FIELD

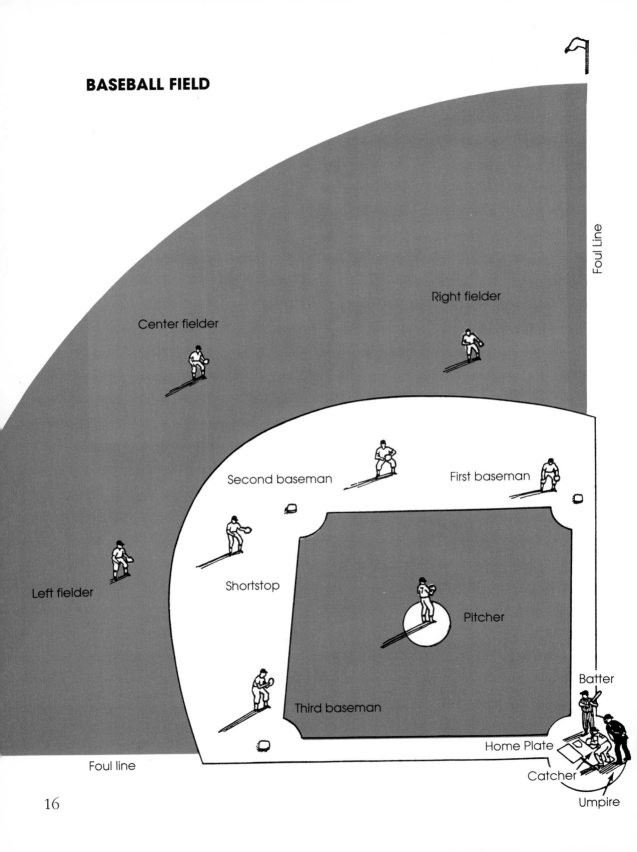

Foul Line

Right fielder

Center fielder

Second baseman

First baseman

Shortstop

Left fielder

Pitcher

Third baseman

Batter

Home Plate

Foul line

Catcher

Umpire

The distance between bases is 60 feet in Little League. High school bases are usually 90 feet apart. They are 90 feet apart in the majors.

The Object of Baseball

There are nine players on each team. Each team takes turns being on offense and defense. The team on offense sends one player at a time to home plate. This player is called a batter. The batter takes part in a showdown with the other team's pitcher. The pitcher stands in the middle of the diamond on the pitcher's mound. The pitcher's teammates are behind and around him or her. They are called fielders. The pitcher throws the baseball toward the catcher. The catcher squats behind home plate. The batter stands alongside home plate in an area called the batter's box. He or she tries to hit the ball with the bat as it goes by.

The batter and his or her teammates try to reach base safely. When they reach base, they are called runners. They try to advance in a counterclockwise direction around the base path. The runners must touch each base in the order first base, then second base, and then third base. The final base is home plate.

Each time a player crosses home plate it is called a "run." The team with the most runs at the end of the game is the winner.

The batter can reach base safely many ways: walk, hit by pitch, base hit, extra-base hit, home run, error, or fielder's choice. The most common way to reach base is by a base hit.

A walk is when the batter gets four balls. The pitcher aims for a strike zone. The strike zone is an imaginary area above home plate. The top of the zone is even with the batter's armpits. The bottom of the zone is even with the batter's knees. If the pitch is outside the strike zone, and the batter does not swing, it is called a ball.

When a batter hits the ball, he or she starts running toward first base. If the batter reaches the base before the defense can get an out, it is a hit. If the batter got to first base, it is called a single. Reaching second base is called a double. Reaching third base is called a triple. Reaching all four bases is called a home run. Hitting the ball over the fence is an automatic home run.

Out at first base

Ready to catch a fly ball

The batter can also reach base on an error. An error is when the batter reaches base because of a mistake by the fielders.

The team stays at bat until they make three outs. Outs can be made in a few different ways: strikeout, fly out, groundout, force-out, or throw out.

The pitcher can strike a batter out. If a batter gets three strikes, the batter is out. A strike is a pitch that the batter swings at and misses. A strike can also be a "called" strike. A called strike is when the batter does not swing and the ball passes through the strike zone. A foul ball is also a strike. A foul ball is one that is hit by the batter but lands outside of the first-base and third-base foul lines. Once the batter has two strikes, a foul ball does not count as a strike. It is then treated as a "do-over."

18

A batter can fly out. That means a fielder catches the ball before it hits the ground. A foul fly ball can also be caught for an out.

The batter can ground out. That means an infielder picked up the ball and threw it to first base. The first baseman must catch the ball before the batter gets there. The first baseman must have a foot on the base when he or she has the ball.

The batter can hit into a force-out. This can happen if a runner is on first base, or runners are on first and second base, or bases are loaded, which means all three bases have runners. The runners must try to advance to the next base if the batter hits a ground ball.

In a force situation, a fielder picks up a ground ball. He or she can get a force-out by throwing the ball to another fielder. That fielder must have a foot on the base that the forced runner is heading to. The fielder must catch the ball before the runner gets there. That is a force-out.

On a force-out, the runner is out. The batter is safe at first base. After getting a force-out, a team can try for a double play.

A double play is when there are two outs on one play. It starts with a force-out. Then the fielder relays the throw to first base. If it beats the batter to first base, it is a double play. Both the runner and the batter are out. Sometimes there is a triple play, or three outs on one play. But that is very rare.

It is different when it is not a force situation. The runner does not have to advance to another base. He or she does so at his or her own risk. To get the runner out, a fielder must tag him or her with the ball or with a glove that has the ball in it. The fielder must tag the runner before the runner reaches a base.

After three outs, the teams switch roles. The batting team goes into the field. The fielding team comes to bat. When each team has made three outs, an inning has been completed. A full game lasts nine innings in the major leagues. It lasts seven innings in high school and six innings in Little League. Extra innings are played to break a tie score.

Now...play ball!

CHAPTER 4

THE PLAYING POSITIONS

In baseball there is a place for everyone. A person's size or shape does not matter. That is one of the reasons it is such a popular game. Baseball is known as America's national pastime.

A player who can play many positions is valuable to the team. That person will probably get to play a lot, more often than someone who is limited to just one position. Here is a look at each of the nine defensive positions.

Pitcher

The pitcher stands on top of the pitcher's mound, a raised circular area in the middle of the infield. He or she throws the ball to a target presented by the catcher. The pitcher's goal is to get the batter out. He or she can get the batter out many ways. The most dramatic way is striking out the batter. The pitcher can also get a batter out on a ground ball or fly ball, or get a force-out on a ground ball.

The pitcher must avoid walks. A walk is also known as a base on balls or a free pass. The batter did not earn his way on. Making a batter earn his way on by swinging the bat is the most important duty of a pitcher.

◄ A pitcher should use a comfortable and natural pitching motion.

A no-hitter is when a pitcher pitches an entire game without allowing a hit. Eight-time All-Star Nolan Ryan pitched his seventh no-hitter in 1991. No other pitcher in major league history has thrown more than four no-hitters. Ryan's historic record should last a long time.

When a pitcher throws a lot of balls, his fielders tend to relax. They can be caught off guard when the batter hits the pitch. When a pitcher is always in the strike zone, his fielders stay alert. They are ready for the action that is about to happen.

Pitching tips: A pitcher should use a comfortable throwing motion. It should also be a natural throwing motion. Start by playing "catch" with your catcher. Then increase the speed. Use the catcher's mitt or chest protector as a target. Do not try to simply reach the target. Try to throw the ball "through" the target. Pretend you want the ball to come out the other side. This will give you a good follow-through after you release the ball. It will give the pitch added speed without throwing as hard as you can.

Here is advice about pitching from a raised mound. Nolan Ryan suggests using the "tall and fall" method. That means to stand straight and well balanced when you begin. Then let yourself fall towards the batter as you throw the ball.

Most pitcher's mounds used by youth leagues are not raised. Pitching from a flat mound is different. The pitcher must drive towards the plate. He or she must push off hard with the back foot while striding forward with the front foot.

Overhand pitches are the easiest to control.

Throwing techniques: There are many "release" points, the position of the arm when the ball is thrown. Overhand is the type of throw that is most recommended. Overhand throws are the easiest to control. They also allow you to have all your body weight behind each pitch. This makes the pitch go faster. It also puts less stress on your arm and shoulder.

There are many types of pitches. Pitchers and their coaches are always coming up with new pitches. Some of the more common types of pitches are fastballs, curveballs, and change-ups.

A fastball is basically a straight ball. But a good fastball will have movement, too. That means it will sink down, appear to rise up, or dart inside or outside.

Some pitchers can throw a knuckleball. A knuckleball has very little spin. It flutters on its way to the batter.

The type of pitch is determined by two things: how the pitcher grips the ball and how he or she throws it. Most pitches are gripped with the index finger and middle finger on or across the seams. The thumb is placed under or alongside the ball. The ball is held loosely. There should be a slight space between the palm and the ball. This gives the ball more spin. More spin gives the pitch more speed and movement.

Hints from the coach: Young players are often advised to throw just straight balls. They should concentrate on throwing strikes. They probably should not begin throwing curveballs until they are 16 years old. The strain on the elbow can cause damage to young players' arms and joints. Major league pitching coach Tom House tells how to avoid such injuries. The key is to throw each pitch correctly.

It is up to the coach to decide what pitches a young player can throw. It is the job of that coach to teach him or her the proper way to throw. It is also the coach's job to make sure the young player does not throw too many pitches. That can be the most important difference between damaging or protecting a young player's arm.

The complete pitcher: The pitcher does more than just throw. The pitcher must be able to field ground balls. He or she must catch line drives, pop-ups, and bunts. The pitcher is involved in pickoff plays. He or she covers first base on ground balls to the first baseman. The pitcher backs up third base and home plate on throws from the outfield.

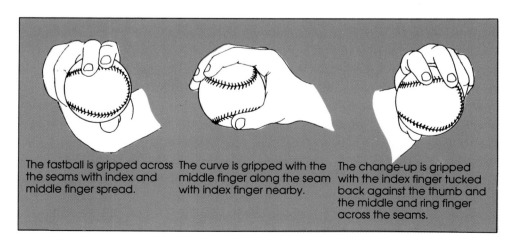

The fastball is gripped across the seams with index and middle finger spread.

The curve is gripped with the middle finger along the seam with index finger nearby.

The change-up is gripped with the index finger tucked back against the thumb and the middle and ring finger across the seams.

The pitcher is the busiest player on the field. He or she can also feel like the loneliest player. All eyes are on the pitcher as he or she prepares to pitch the ball in a key situation. It is a big responsibility. There is a lot of pressure. Good pitchers stay calm. They must control their pitches, and they must control their emotions.

Catchers must be tough and smart.

Catcher

Catcher can be one of the most fun positions. It is a very busy and difficult position. Also, it is sometimes painful.

The catcher's main job is to catch the balls thrown by the pitcher. First he or she must give the pitcher a good target. The catcher squats behind home plate. He or she holds the catcher's glove in the strike zone. The catcher can give the pitcher a secret sign. This tells the pitcher which type of pitch to throw.

The catcher must also be able to catch pop-ups. He or she must pick up and throw bunted balls. In older leagues the catcher must also throw out runners attempting to steal a base.

You notice two things about a catcher before a pitch is even thrown. The first is that the catcher is the only defensive player who is not looking in toward home plate. The catcher is the only defensive player who is looking out at the field. He or she sees the field the same way the batter sees it. The catcher can see if defensive teammates have shifted out of position. He or she can then warn teammates. The catcher must keep teammates aware of how many outs there are. He or she raises the right number of fingers while yelling out the situation.

You will also notice the catcher wears outer protective equipment. This guards against foul tips and other hazards. A foul tip is a ball that is only slightly tipped by the batter. Foul tips often hit the catcher in the mask, chest protector, or shin guard. Catchers should protect their throwing hand by making a fist behind their back during the pitch.

The catcher's extra equipment also comes in handy at other times. It helps when he or she tries to block pitches in the dirt. It also gives protection when a runner is sliding into home. You will see runners crash into catchers on television. In youth leagues runners must slide on close plays.

Catchers must be tough but also smart. They must know the rules and be alert about the situation. Catchers must always keep their teammates informed.

First Baseman

The first baseman receives throws from infielders after they field a grounder. He or she must catch the throw and step on first base before the batter reaches the base. Then the batter is out.

The first baseman wears a special glove. It is a cross between a catcher's glove and a fielder's glove. It helps him or her scoop low throws out of the dirt. It also helps snag throws that sail off target.

First baseman

The first baseman must be able to field ground balls and get pop-ups and line drives. He or she must always be ready to come in to field a bunt. A bunt is a lightly hit ball. The batter does not take a full swing. The ball travels only a few feet in front of home plate.

The first baseman must be sure-handed. He or she has to catch a lot of throws. Some will be off-line or bounce in the dirt. The first baseman has to field a lot of ground balls. Teams always put one of their best "glove men" at first base.

Second baseman

Second Baseman

The second baseman and the shortstop are the team's middle infielders. Most ground balls go to either the second baseman or shortstop. These players must be the team's best fielding infielders. They must be sure-handed on ground balls. They must be able to move quickly to either side. They must make good throws to first base. But the second baseman's arm does not have to be as strong as the shortstop's.

All infielders should be ready to "improvise," or do whatever it takes to get the runner out. Overhand throws are the strongest and easiest to control. But sometimes infielders must hurry to get a speedy runner. There may be no time to straighten up to make an overhand throw. They have to scoop the ball and throw it in the same motion.

Accuracy is also important. Accuracy means making the ball go where you want. A rushed throw often goes wild. That allows the runners to take an extra base. A more careful throw may not get the runner out. But it does not give him or her any extra bases.

The second baseman is also involved in cutoff plays on throws from the outfield. The second baseman can go halfway out to right field to be a relay man. That means he or she catches the outfielder's throw then throws it to the infield. The second baseman can stay in the infield to cover second base. He or she also covers the base on steals and force plays and is involved in double plays. The second baseman will be either the "pivot man" or the player starting the double play. The pivot man receives the throw at second base for the first out. Then he or she throws to first base for the second out. It can be a difficult play for the second baseman. The second baseman must throw across his or her body. That makes it hard to get speed on the throw.

Shortstop

Shortstops have all the duties described for second basemen. The shortstop also is considered the captain of the infield. He or she is a skilled and graceful fielder and can get to balls that most players cannot reach. The shortstop has a strong arm. Shortstops also must always be aware of what is happening on the field. They must communicate, or talk, to their teammates. They must be loud enough for all of their teammates to hear. They must shout these instructions quickly before it is too late.

Shortstops are quick with their hands and feet. They must also be quick with their wits. The shortstop tells the other fielders how many

The shortstop, captain of the infield, often covers second base against runners.

outs there are. He or she also helps the team avoid confusion. For example, on a pop-up more than one fielder might be able to make the catch. The shortstop tells which player to catch it. He or she also controls where the throws from the outfield go by shouting to the outfielders. The shortstop and the second baseman talk on cutoff plays and double plays. They decide who will cover the base.

The shortstop has an advantage as the pivot man. The shortstop takes the throw from the second baseman and moves across the "bag" and toward first base. This is a natural motion. It helps the shortstop get more speed on the throw.

Third baseman

Third Baseman

Third base is also known as the "hot corner." Batted balls often come there very quickly. Third basemen do not have to be fast runners. But they must have quick reactions. They must be able to quickly move the glove. They must be able to quickly take one or two steps to either side. Great third basemen are able to dive to field ground balls. They quickly bounce back to their feet then still throw the runner or batter out. A strong, accurate arm is a must for any third baseman.

The ball comes to the third baseman very quickly. Coaches tell their third baseman to "just knock the ball down." The third baseman usually still will have time to throw the batter out. Third basemen must be ready for a hot smash. But they also must rush in on a bunt. It can be scary. Imagine rushing in for a bunt when the batter is actually swinging away.

It takes a lot of nerve to play third base. The third baseman must always be alert. The glove must be ready in front of him or her. The third baseman must be ready for anything that might happen.

Left Fielder

Left field requires a player with a lot of speed. The left fielder must also have the reactions of an infielder. All outfielders must be able to catch fly balls. They also must keep bouncing balls from becoming extra-base hits. The left fielder's arm does not have to be as strong as the other outfielders'. The left fielder's throws are shorter. Second base and third base are right in front of him or her. A strong arm is helpful on throws to home. But the left fielder can use the cutoff play. The relay man will get the ball home quickly.

The left fielder must "back up" the center fielder. This happens on any ball hit to center field. The left fielder must race over and get behind the center fielder. He or she must be ready to make the play in case the ball gets past the center fielder.

Left fielder

Center Fielder

The center fielder should be the best all-around outfielder on the team. The center fielder is considered the captain of the outfield. He or she is the outfielder with the most speed. The center fielder has the most ground to cover. The center fielder must also have a very strong arm. He or she has to make long throws and move like a cat. The center fielder must be able to quickly run in, run back, or run to either side.

All fielders must "call the ball" before trying to catch a fly ball or pop-up. You call the ball by shouting "I got it." This avoids confusion. It prevents fielders from running into each other.

Center fielder

The center fielder helps with calling out who will catch the fly balls. But it is also baseball tradition that the center fielder should take charge. He or she should try to catch any fly ball he can reach. The other outfielders run for fly balls until they hear the center fielder "call them off."

Center field is fun. It is also a very important position. Some of the best players in history played center field. Willie Mays, Mickey Mantle, and Joe DiMaggio were center fielders. Ken Griffey, Jr., is one of today's most exciting players. He is a center fielder.

Right fielder

Right Fielder

The outfielder with the strongest arm usually plays right field. The right fielder has to make the longest throws. It is a long throw from right field to third base. It is a long way to home plate. The right fielder must also be able to make difficult throws to second base. Sometimes the right fielder is running away from the base when he or she fields the ball.

The throws are long and difficult. The right fielder often needs help from the cutoff man. Right fielders who can throw far are very valuable. Hall of Famer Roberto Clemente was an All-Star 12 times. He was a great hitter. But he is just as famous for his powerful arm.

Designated Hitter

The designated hitter is also called the "DH." The DH is not a fielding position. It was first included in the American League portion of the major leagues in 1973. It allows a player to be a batter

Hits create runs. Runs win ball games.

without having to play defense. The designated hitter is used in almost all youth leagues. It is also used in high schools and colleges. The National League portion of the major leagues, however, does not use the designated hitter.

THROWING AND CATCHING

Throwing a ball is a natural motion. It begins when an infant tosses its rattle or bottle. After that, it is just a matter of practice. You can learn to throw a ball exactly where you want it to go.

Throwing

Pick up the ball. Use the hand that feels most comfortable for throwing. The throwing hand is nearly always the same hand you use to brush your teeth. It is best to throw the ball with your fingertips on its seams. The seams are also called stitches. This gives you a better grip on the ball. It creates more spin when you throw it. The spin will allow you to throw with more speed. It also gives you better control.

To make the throw, first bring your arm back. Cock your arm by bending your elbow. Your throwing hand and the ball should be just behind your ear. You are now like a gun. It too is cocked before firing. Now it is time to pull the trigger. Bring your arm quickly forward. Push off hard with your back leg. The back leg is on the same side of your body as your throwing arm. Step with your front leg in the direction of your target. When the front leg lands, release the ball. Try to get your body weight behind the throw.

◄ The pitcher is winding up to throw a fast ball.

Follow through with the throwing arm after you have released the ball. This will help your control. Pretend that you are trying to throw your hand to the target. Try to throw the ball through the target not just to the target.

Warm up before throwing hard: It is important to warm up before throwing hard or throwing far. Start by standing close to a teammate. Softly toss the ball. Then slowly increase the distance between you and your teammate.

Try not to throw in cold or damp weather. This is when many arm injuries occur. But sometimes you must throw in those conditions. Give yourself extra time to warm up. You do not want to hurt your arm, elbow, or shoulder. And wear proper clothes for the weather. Long sleeves should be worn in cold, damp weather.

Catching

There are two important rules in learning to catch a baseball. Keep your eyes on the ball, and have "soft" hands. Do not try to catch a ball with stiff hands. The ball might bounce out of the glove. Soft hands will cushion the thrown or batted ball. That will make catching the ball easier. To have soft hands, you must bring the ball in toward you. If you stab at the ball, you will knock it out of your glove.

Fielding

Ground balls: Ground balls should be scooped up with two hands. You should be moving toward the ground ball. Gather up the ball in a down-to-up motion. The glove should start below the ball and come up. It is easier to bring the hands up quickly for a bad bounce. It is harder to drop the hands down if you start high and the ball skips low. When fielding a ground ball, you should look like a monkey. Your arms should hang to the ground. You should make a swooping motion toward the ground ball.

Fly balls: Outfielders must learn to figure out where a fly ball is headed. That is called "judging" a fly ball. Then the outfielder can

Ken Griffey, Jr., judging a fly ball for a catch. ▶

run to the spot the ball is headed. He or she will be there waiting for it when it comes down. Outfielders should try to move in when they catch the ball. They will be able to make a stronger throw. Most fly balls and high pop-ups "carry." That means they travel farther than they at first seem to be going. Go back a little farther than you think you need to. Be ready to come back in if the ball does not "carry."

CHAPTER 6

BATTING AND BASERUNNING

Don Mattingly has been banging out hits for the New York Yankees since 1982. He brought a .311 lifetime batting average into the 1993 season. It was his 11th year in the major leagues. Mattingly has been an All-Star six times. Mattingly's fine stroke did not happen by magic. He worked very hard to become such a good hitter. He still works hard to stay a good hitter. Here is the Yankees' star's secret.

Batting

"First, you should pick up a bat you can handle, one that's not too heavy," says Mattingly. "The bat should be light enough so you can swing it easily. Grab it in a way that feels comfortable in your hands. Next, take a shoulder-width stance. Your feet should be a comfortable distance apart, not too wide and not too close together."

Raise the bat. Your hands should be even with your back shoulder. Raise your hands a little higher if that feels right to you. Starting with the hands high prevents an uppercut swing. You must always swing level or down on the ball. Never swing up.

◄ Don Mattingly of the New York Yankees demonstrating the correct way to hit the ball

39

Always try to hit line drives or hard ground balls. Never try to hit fly balls or home runs. Home runs come from solid contact not from uppercut swinging for the fences.

It is always better to hit ground balls than fly balls. Fly balls need only one play to be an out. The fielder just has to catch the ball. Ground balls need three plays for an out: catching the grounder, throwing to first base, and then having the first baseman catch the ball. The defense has three chances to make a mistake. Then the batter is safe.

> ## A DON MATTINGLY TIP
>
> "You have to see the ball. Just keep your eyes on the ball. See it and hit it. Watch the ball. Train your head to stay down. Your eyes will tell you where to go with the bat."
>
> "There is nothing wrong with swinging hard. But do not try to kill the ball. Keep your head still. Keep your eyes on the ball and swing hard."

See it and hit it: You are standing ready in the batter's box. Now you must closely watch the pitcher and his or her pitch.

Sometimes you will have trouble against a pitcher. Sometimes the bat feels too heavy, and there is not a lighter one. Then the batter should "choke up" on the bat. Choking up means to move your hands a little further up the bat handle. That will make the bat easier to swing. Choking up will give you better contact. But it will also take away some of the power.

How to become a good hitter: Don Mattingly says hitting off a batting tee is good practice. A tee is a rubber pipe that stands about waist-high. The ball is placed on the top of the pipe. Before every game at Yankee Stadium, Mattingly spends time hitting off a tee.

"Hitting the ball off a tee makes you keep your head down," says Mattingly. "It makes you watch the ball. It makes you keep your eye on the ball. To hit a ball off a tee you have to have a level swing."

Baserunning

After hitting the ball, the batter becomes a runner. Getting safely to first base is the first goal. Always run as hard as you can all the way to first base. Do not look where the ball was hit. Do not watch the fielders. Your coach just outside of first base will tell you what to do.

Run hard all the way, even if you think it is going to be an easy out. The fielder might drop the ball. That would make a batter safe if he or she was running hard all the way. The first rule of baserunning is go until the coach tells you to stop. Always listen to your coaches. They will tell you what to do on the base paths.

There is a coach outside first base. There is also a coach in foul ground outside third base. Watch the first base coach until you head for second. Then look to the third base coach for instructions the rest of the way.

Sliding is an important skill.

Rounding the Base: Do not wait until you get to the base to start your turn. Run straight toward a base. But about 15 feet before you reach the base, go a little to your right. Then start turning left. You can cut easily across the base. Touch the inside corner of the base. Then go full speed to the next base.

Speed is basic to good baserunning. Good judgment and quick reactions are even more important. You need good judgment to size up the situation. You must know the number of outs. You must know the outfielder's arm strength. You need quick reactions to take advantage of a chance to advance.

HOW TO KEEP SCORE

Keeping track of a game in a score book is fun. It is also a way to remember a special game. A score book shows every play in a game. Everything goes on one page.

Keeping score is made easier by giving a number to each position in the field. These numbers are not the numbers on the uniforms, which change. These numbers are for positions. They never change. The numbers are:

1-Pitcher	4-Second baseman	7-Left fielder
2-Catcher	5-Third baseman	8-Center fielder
3-First baseman	6-Shortstop	9-Right fielder

Each batter's progress is noted in boxes next to his or her name. There is a box for each inning. Sometimes the batter makes no progress. That is noted in the center of the box. A swinging strikeout is recorded as a "K." A strikeout looking, or a called strikeout, is recorded as a backward "K." For a fly out, just record the position number of the fielder who caught the ball. A fly out to left field is recorded as "F7," or just "7." If the batter grounded out, the fielders are noted. Write them in the order of the play. A groundout to shortstop, who throws to first base, is recorded as "6-3."

Sometimes a batter reaches base. It is noted in that player's box for that inning. A walk is shown as "BB." That is short for base on balls. An error by the shortstop is "E6." A single is one long dash in that box: "—." A double is noted by two dashes, one above the other: "=." For a home run, four dashes, or the letters "HR," are written into the scorecard.

When a player scores, a filled-in diamond is drawn. It goes in the player's box for that inning. This shows that the player has scored. It makes it easy to see how many runs were scored.

The most important thing is to tell what happened. Do not guess at what numbers to write. If you are not sure, write it in words. When in doubt, write it out. Just write "Out" for a batter making an out. Write "Single" for a batter getting a single.

Bill White is the National League president. Phil Rizzuto used to be shortstop for the New York Yankees. For years they were partners in the Yankees' broadcast booth. During one game, Bill White was going to get some coffee. He passed his score book to Rizzuto. He asked Rizzuto to keep score for him while he was gone. White returned three batters later. He looked at the score book. Next to the three batters' names was written, in order, "6-3, F7, WW." Bill White turned to Phil Rizzuto and asked, "WW? What the heck is WW?" Rizzuto replied: "Wasn't Watching."

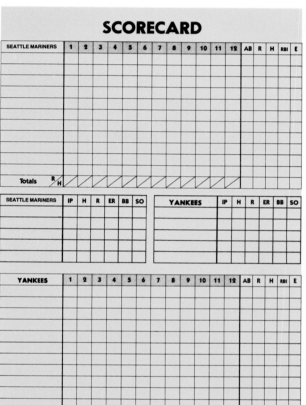

A typical scorecard

COACHES AND MANAGERS

There are adults in charge of youth teams. They are called managers and coaches. Sometimes the manager is called the head coach. The head coach acts as a teacher and a general. His or her job as a teacher is to help young players improve their skills. As a general, the head coach's job is to get all of the players working together as a team.

The head coach makes a plan to use against the other team. That plan includes making out the lineup. The lineup shows the batting order. It also shows who will play each position. The coach does what he or she thinks is best for the whole team, not just for one person.

Umpires: The umpire is like a policeman on the field. It is the umpire's job to make sure the rules are followed. The umpire decides if a pitch is a ball or a strike. Sometimes there are very close plays. That is when an umpire is most important. He or she has to decide whether the player was safe or out. The umpire's decision is final. Players should not argue with an umpire. The manager or coach can ask the umpire to explain the call. The umpire starts the game with the words "Play ball!" During the game, the umpire is in charge. He or she has the power to throw a player or coach out of

Treat your opponents with respect. ▶

the game. The umpire will do this for unsportsmanlike conduct. Unsportsmanlike conduct includes arguing with the umpire, running into a player on purpose, throwing equipment, or using foul language.

Sportsmanship: Treat all members of the game with respect. That means your teammates, your coaches, the other team, and the umpire. Play hard. But do not lose your temper. Do not throw equipment or use foul language. And never try to hurt anyone.

Young players are often told that it is not winning or losing that counts. It is how you play the game that is most important. That is true. But most people still feel badly when they lose. The best cure for that bad feeling is lots of practice. The more you practice, the better you will play. You will enjoy playing more. And then the wins will come.

Always remember that things can change in a hurry. In 1990, the Minnesota Twins and the Atlanta Braves were in last place. The very next year, they played each other in the World Series.

Do not forget the words of New York Yankees All-Star Don Mattingly. "The most important thing is to have fun when you are playing ball."

GLOSSARY

Bag: Another name for a base

Bases loaded: When there are runners on first, second, and third bases

Batter's box: The area alongside home plate in which the batter stands awaiting the pitch

Bunt: A lightly hit ball, without a full swing, that travels only a few feet in front of home plate

Change-up: A pitch disguised to look like a fastball while the pitcher is winding up. It actually travels much slower than a fastball. It can cause a batter who is expecting a fastball to swing too early.

Cleanup hitter: The player who bats fourth in the batting order. This is usually a player who can hit with power. The cleanup hitter often gets up with a chance to drive in runners.

Counterclockwise: The direction opposite the direction in which the hands of a clock move. The runners advance around the bases in a counterclockwise direction.

Cutoff man: Also known as the relay man. This player is usually an infielder. He or she stands halfway between the outfielder who has the ball, and the base, to which the outfielder intends to throw the ball. The cutoff man cuts off the throw and relays it to the intended base.

Diamond: The infield portion of the baseball field. It is outlined by the base path, which is in the shape of a diamond.

Double play: When the team in the field gets two outs on one play. Sometimes the team in the field is able to make a triple play. That is three outs on one play.

Extra innings: If the score is tied at the end of the regular number of innings (for example, six innings in Little League, nine innings in major leagues), the game continues into extra innings. All regular baseball rules are followed, and both teams get an equal chance to bat until one team wins.

Fielder's choice: When a batter reaches first base safely, but one of the runners is forced out on the play

Hot corner: Third base is called the hot corner because right-handed batters often smash the ball in that direction.

Leading: When a runner edges a few steps away from the base before or during a pitch to the batter

Pickoff play: When a pitcher throws to one of his infielders to try to catch a runner who is leading from a base instead of pitching to the batter

Pitcher's mound: An area in the middle of the diamond, usually slightly raised, from which the pitcher throws the ball to his catcher

Strike zone: The target area that a pitcher aims for. When a pitch passes through the area above home plate and, at the same time, between the batter's armpits and knees, the pitch is called a strike if the batter does not swing at it.

MORE WORDS TO KNOW

Grand slam: When a batter hits a home run with the bases loaded

Ground rules: Special rules that apply to the field you are using. For example, if there is a hole in the outfield fence, a ground rule could be made that any ball that goes through the hole counts as a double. In the major leagues, any fair ball that bounces over the outfield wall is a ground-rule double. Ground rules must be decided before the game.

Leadoff batter: The first batter in the lineup or the first batter of an inning

Pinch hitter: A substitute batter. In the major leagues, when a substitute enters the game, the player he replaced cannot return to the game. In most youth leagues the original player can return to the game.

Relief pitcher: Any pitcher who enters later in the game

Rubber: A slab of rubber in the middle of the pitcher's

mound. The pitcher must have one foot on the rubber when he or she makes a pitch.

Sacrifice fly: When a runner scores after tagging up, the fly out is called a sacrifice fly.

Tagging up: After a fly ball is caught for an out (but not the third out), any runner on base can try to advance only after the fly ball is caught.

FURTHER READING

Aylesworth, Thomas G. *The Kid's World Almanac of Baseball*. Pharos, 1990

Baseball: You Call the Play. Western, 1992

Baseball Encyclopedia. Macmillan, 1991

Bloom, Marc. *Baseball*. Scholastic, 1991

Carroll, Bob. *The Major League Way to Play Baseball*. Simon and Schuster, 1991

INDEX